Countries of the World

Japan

by Michael Dahl

Reading Consultant:
Ichiro Tange
Japan Informational Culture Center
Embassy of Japan

Bridgestone Books
an Imprint of Capstone Press

Bridgestone Books are published by Capstone Press
818 North Willow Street, Mankato, Minnesota 56001
Copyright © 1997 by Capstone Press
All rights reserved
Printed in the United States of America

Library of Congress Cataloging-in-Publication Data
Dahl, Michael.
   Japan/by Michael Dahl.
   p. cm.--(Bridgestone countries of the world)
   Includes bibliographical references and index.
   Summary: An introduction to the geography, history, people, and culture of the island
country of Japan.
   ISBN 1-56065-524-0
   1. Japan--Juvenile literature. [1. Japan.]   I. Title.
  II. Series: Countries of the world (Mankato, Minn.)
DS806.D323   1997
915.2--dc21

                    96-39691
                    CIP
                    AC

Photo credits
Flag Research Center, 5 (left)
FPG/7, 14; Guy Marche, 5 (right); Jean Kugler, 8; Stan Osolinski, 12;
  Dave Bartruff, 18
International Stock/Miwako Ikeda, cover
Unicorn/Kimberly Burnham, 10; Brent Flipper, 16; FCF Earney, 20

Table of Contents

Fast Facts

Official Name: Nihon (nih-HOHN)
Capital: Tokyo
Population: 125 million
Language: Japanese
Religions: Buddhism, Shintoism

Size: 145,850 square miles (379,210 square kilometers) *Twenty-five Japans would fit into the United States.*

Major Crop: Rice

Maps

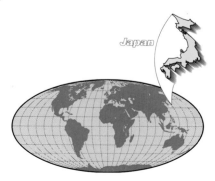

4

Flag

Japan's flag is white with a big red dot in the middle.

Japan is called the land of the rising sun. The red dot stands for the sun without its rays.

Currency

The Japanese currency is called yen. A hole cut in the middle of a yen makes it lucky. Then it is called a lucky yen.

The number of yen it takes to equal one U.S. dollar changes daily.

A Country of Many Islands

The Pacific Ocean surrounds Japan's islands. Japan has four main islands and many small islands. Some islands are connected by bridges.

More than 125 million people live in Japan. Most Japanese people live in big cities. This is because forests and mountains cover three-fourths of the islands.

Many of Japan's mountains are volcanoes. Mount Fuji is Japan's most famous volcano. Volcanoes are holes in the crust of the earth. They can erupt, or blow up.

Japan has survived many floods, earthquakes, and erupting volcanoes. Some Japanese buildings are built to be able to wave back and forth. That way they will not fall apart during an earthquake.

Mount Fuji is Japan's most famous volcano.

Going to School

Japanese children go to school five days a week. Twice a month they attend school on Saturday. Many schools require uniforms. Some schools even make boys shave their heads.

Working together is very important to Japanese people. Students learn teamwork. Everyday they clean their school. They keep the rooms, halls, toilets, and yards neat.

Students must pass a difficult test to get into high school. At night, many children go to a special school called juku (JOO-koo). At juku, they study the subjects that give them trouble in regular school. This helps them do better on the high-school test.

Many Japanese schools require uniforms.

A Culture of Respect

Millions of people are crowded together on Japan's small islands. Japanese people must share space. People get along by using good manners. Parents, teachers, and older people receive special respect.

Japanese people do not shake hands. They greet one another by bowing. Bowing shows respect. Children learn the right way to bow.

Important people receive deep, long bows. Japanese bow when thanking someone, too. Stores have greeters who stand by the doors. They bow to people who shop at the store.

Japanese people have many festivals. This is how they show respect for their land and religion. Dragon or lion dances are a popular part of the celebrations.

The dragon dance is popular at many festivals.

Animals

Each of Japan's islands looks different. Northern islands are colder. They have a lot of snow and ice. Many animals live there.

Snow monkeys chatter in the trees. Brown bears come into villages looking for food. Raccoon dogs sleep in caves all winter.

Japan's southern islands are warmer. Deer live in grassy fields. Wild boars roam the mountains. A boar is a wild pig. Giant lizards creep through the jungles.

Different birds fly over Japan looking for fish to eat. Japanese people believe the crane brings them good luck. A crane is a large bird. It has a long neck and bill and long legs.

Some Japanese children keep pet dogs and cats. Busy cities have ponds where people fish during lunch.

Japanese people believe the crane brings good luck.

13

Tokyo and Trains

Tokyo (toh-KYOH) is the capital of Japan. Nearly one-fourth of all Japanese people live in or near Tokyo. This giant city is made up of 40 small cities squeezed together.

Freeways stretch from one end of Japan to the other. Subways and trains move people around Tokyo.

Trains are very full. Special city workers help people squeeze into the trains. They push and shove passengers. That way more people can crowd into the train cars.

Japan has the fastest trains in the world. They are called bullet trains. Bullet trains travel 130 miles (208 kilometers) per hour. Some even zoom through underwater tunnels.

Japan's bullet trains are the fastest in the world.

Japanese Sports

Sumo (SOO-moh) wrestling is Japan's national sport. Sumo wrestlers weigh more than 300 pounds (135 kilograms). Still, they are flexible enough to do the splits. A sumo match lasts about 30 seconds. The wrestlers try to shove each other out of a small circle on the floor.

Children in school look forward to Sports Day. On that day, they can compete in different events. Students try hard to win races, relays, and piggyback fights.

Japanese people also enjoy baseball. Many cities have a team. In October, there is a big playoff game called the Japan Series.

Pachinko (pah-CHEENK-oh) is a favorite Japanese game. It is like a pinball game. But instead of one ball, pachinko uses thousands of balls.

Sumo wrestling matches last about 30 seconds.

At Home

Most Japanese people live in crowded cities. Their homes have small rooms. Many Japanese also live in tall apartment buildings.

Japanese people take off their shoes by the door. This is because their floors are covered with tatami (TAH-tah-mee) mats. These mats are made of grass and can tear easily.

At home, some Japanese sit on cushions at low tables. At night, many sleep on futons (FOO-tahns). Futons are mats that roll out.

Japanese children usually wear American clothes. They wear jeans, T-shirts, and sneakers. Businesspeople wear suits.

Once Japanese men and women wore robes made of colored silk. These robes were called kimonos (ki-MOH-nohs). Today kimonos are worn only on special holidays.

Kimonos are worn only on special holidays.

Fish and Rice

Seafood is a popular Japanese food. Octopus, shark, and fish live off the coast of Japan. Fishing boats catch many sea creatures. Japan also has fish farms. These farms raise fish to sell.

Rice is part of every meal. It is Japan's biggest crop. Farmers use every bit of land to grow rice. Rice is even grown on mountainsides.

In Japan, some meals are not cooked. Fish is sometimes eaten raw. Sushi (SOO-shee) is a popular Japanese meal. Raw fish is put over cold, cooked rice.

Japanese eat with chopsticks. Chopsticks are two sticks used to pick up food. Food is arranged to look beautiful on the plates. Japanese people enjoy both the taste and the appearance of food.

Japanese people enjoy food's taste and appearance.

Hands On: Make a Sand Garden

Japanese people love gardens, even without flowers. A garden is a good place to be alone and relax.

Japanese people show respect to things as well as to people. Rocks, water, and sand are important parts of nature.

What You Need

A box lid
Sand or gravel
Three different sizes of rocks
A comb or tiny rake

What You Do

1. Fill the box lid with your sand or gravel. Make sure the sand covers the whole inside of the lid.
2. Place your rocks in the sand. Think of the rocks as islands sitting in the sea. You can arrange the rocks any way you like.
3. Take your comb or tiny rake and rake the sand. Make ridges in the sand. The ridges will look like waves in the ocean. Straight lines stand for calm water. Wavy lines stand for moving water.
4. You can make circle shapes with your comb. Circles in a sand garden look like raindrops hitting the water.

Learn to Speak Japanese

excuse me	sumimasen	(soo-mee-MAH-sen)
goodbye	sayonara	(sye-YAH-nor-ah)
hello	konnichiwa	(koh-nee-CHEE-wah)
How are you?	Ogenki deska?	(oh-GEN-kee DESK-ah)
I'm fine	Genki desu.	(GEN-kee DES-oo)
no	iie	(ee-A)
please	onegai shimasu	(OH-neg-eye shee-MAH-soo)
thank you	domo arigato	(doh-MOH ah-ree-GAH-toh)
yes	hai	(HYE)

Words to Know

boar (BOR)—a wild pig

bullet trains (BUL-it TRANE)—special trains in Japan that go up to 130 miles (208 kilometers) per hour

juku (JOO-koo)—a special school Japanese students attend after regular school

pachinko (pah-CHEENK-oh)—a game like pinball that uses thousands of balls

sumo (SOO-moh)—a type of wrestling where wrestlers try to shove each other out of a small circle on the floor

sushi (SOO-shee)—a meal of raw fish and cold, cooked rice

volcano (vohl-CAY-noh)—a hole in the crust of the earth that can erupt, or blow up

Read More

Cobb, Vicki. *This Place Is Crowded*. New York: Walker and Company, 1992.
Jacobsen, Karen. *Japan*. Danbury, Conn.: Children's Press, 1982.
Kalman, Bobbie. *Japan, the Land*. New York: Crabtree Publishing, 1989.
Kuklin, Susan. *Kodomo, Children of Japan*. New York: G.P. Putnam's Sons, 1995.

Useful Addresses and Internet Sites

Embassy of Japan
2520 Massachusetts Avenue NW
Washington, DC 20008

Pen Pal Planet
P.O. Box 20111
Scranton, PA 18502

Kids Web Japan
http://jin.jcic.or.jp/kidsweb
Kid's Window to Japan
http://jw.stanford.edu:80/KIDS/kids_home.html
World Safari: Japan
http://www.supersurf.com/japan

Index